UNCOMMON COURAGE

IN ACTION

UNCOMMON COURAGE

IN ACTION

THE WORKBOOK

ANDREA T EDWARDS

Copyright © 2021 by Andrea T Edwards
Edited by Joanne Flinn, Authority Services
Graphics by Tim Hamons
Layout by Karl Hunt
Cover by Arewa Lanre
Published by Courageous Publishing

This publication is presented to provide competent and reliable information
regarding the subject matter presented. However, the author and publisher
are not engaged in offering it as legal, financial, health or other professional
advice.

The contents of this book are personal opinions and observations, based on
the author's personal experience. Neither the author or the publisher shall
be held liable or responsible to any person or entity with respect to any loss,
incidental or consequential damages caused, or alleged to have been caused,
directly or indirectly, by the information or programs contained herein. The
advice and strategies contained herein may not be suitable for your situation.
No one should make any decision without first consulting his or her own
professional and conducting his or her own research and due diligence.
You are solely responsible for the consequences of your use of this material.

First edition: June 2021

The publisher is not responsible for the websites (or their content) that are
not owned by the publisher.

Library of Congress Cataloging-in-Publication Data.
Names: Andrea T Edwards, author
Title: Uncommon Courage, An invitation
Identifiers: ISBN 978-1-7372944-0-5 (international print edition)
              ISBN 978-1-7372944-1-2 (digital edition)
Subject: Personal Development, Sustainability, Career Advice

This book is dedicated to my two sons, Lex and Jax.

All I want for you boys (and all children) is a life where you can fully express yourselves and love the world you live in. A world in balance with Mother Nature. I want you to swim in clean oceans and rivers, walk trash-free mountain paths, and breath in crystal-clean air. I want for you to see and experience animals flourishing in the wild, to know peace and harmony, and understand that we must work together for the good of all. I want yours to be a world where all have the opportunity to live with dignity. I hope you'll feel the deep love that must exist within you and within all of us to make this possible. I love you guys. Go and be spreaders of love in the world and never stop fighting for what is right for all life on this planet xxxx

For every book you buy, I plant a tree!

CONTENTS

CONTENTS

INTRODUCTION

WELCOME TO *Uncommon Courage In Action*. I am so pleased you have downloaded or purchased this workbook, because it means you got value from *Uncommon Courage* itself and the stories in it. You'll extend that value as you capture your thoughts and ideas here.

I suggest using this workbook to really think, ponder, and consider what you have been holding onto that isn't serving you anymore—which can include the people in your life.

I know that's not an easy one, but this is about living your best life, as well as finding joy and contentment in your days.

I know it's possible to achieve, and the only way to get there is to take care of ourselves as a priority. This is our opportunity to declutter our minds from the baggage of ideas and emotions that are redundant.

Think of it as the Marie Kondo for the mind, heart, and soul.

When you write a book like *Uncommon Courage*, the real reward is knowing that it helped someone like you live lighter in the world.

Of course, I'd love to know my words are good enough to reach many and help many live lighter, because if we can, we can hit a tipping point where real societal change is possible. This is the sort of change that can help us build a new world—where dignity for all life on earth is at the center of what we design.

If you haven't already, please do come and join the Facebook group Uncommon Courage. Just scan this QR code and it will take you right there.

SCAN ME

Promise me one thing when you get there. Be active! Get involved, interact with posts and other members. Share your insights, epiphanies, opportunities, needs and challenges. I won't stop working there to build a community for you where we commit to supporting and inspiring each other.

Before I leave you to get into courageous action, could you help this movement reach more people? If you have loved and valued the book, would you kindly leave a review on Amazon or wherever you write book reviews? The reality is, book reviews make a massive difference to a book succeeding or not, so it will be a huge gift to me in helping me get the word out. It may be your gift forward to light the path for the next person who is looking for this message.

With that, enjoy filling in these pages and digging into the recesses of your mind, heart, and soul.

Taking courageous action can be hard sometimes, and there will be moments (short or long) where you just can't do it. Go easy on yourself. Step away from your objectives for long as you need to, then come back when you're ready.

My own case study was not linear—it was back and forth, up and down, screaming and laughing. That's life. We're all complex creatures.

I wish you nothing but the best in life and look forward to seeing you in the Uncommon Courage community soon. Let's join hands and build a better world!

With love

Andrea T Edwards

#3

NEVER BE ASHAMED OF THE MUSIC YOU LOVE

SELF-EMPOWERMENT

IF YOU WERE STRANDED ON AN ISLAND, what five songs would you select to keep you company? What do you like about how they make you feel?

1. _____
   _____

2. _____
   _____

3. _____
   _____

4. _____
   _____

5. _____
   _____

#4

DO YOU HAVE VOICES IN YOUR HEAD?

SELF-AWARENESS

O VERCOME THOSE VOICES IN YOUR HEAD.

HERE IS HOW I DID IT.

Step 1: Watch what's going on in your mind. Getting an *awareness* of the voice is half the battle. Notice how you let it be the boss, and how unkind it is to you. Notice how you believe it. It's now time to look at it as something separate, another consciousness.

Can you see this voice? Yes? Well….

Step 2: Shut it down. My voice was very negative to me, and I've learned I must tell it to go away and keep telling it to go until it's gone.

Step 3: Stay on top of it. I'm serious about this part—it can reappear powerfully. If that voice reappears for you, as it may well, identify it again, tell it to go away in strong language, ignore it, and shut it back in its box immediately! Rinse and repeat.

FOLLOW UP ON THAT VOICE

Do you have this negative voice? (circle what is true for you)

Yes   No

What does your voice say to you? Close your eyes and spend time in silence. Ask yourself, what is my negative voice? Work hard to identify it. This can be tricky. The voice may be negative towards self, or it can be negative towards others or circumstances. All three make life worse. Write down what you know.

If not, do you know someone who struggles with it? (circle what is true for you)

Yes   No

If you answered yes, copy this chapter and send it to them (author's permission granted).

Now write what you'll say to that voice every time it appears. *I urge strong language, which can be *very* empowering when used for your own greater good!*

Check in 30 days later. Have you succeeded in identifying that negative voice? Have you shut it down? Remember, if it doesn't serve you, if it makes your life worse (through hatred of self or hatred of others), then break free of it.

Mark your calendar with a monthly check-in for the next 12 months. It will keep trying to come back. It's the very definition of pernicious. DO NOT believe it. It's wrong. If you have an internal voice that makes you feel less or unworthy, it is NEVER right. Shut it down.

Also do check out **PositiveIntelligence.com**. I have been really impressed with what I've seen of the work Shirzad Chamine is doing. His work will help you overcome your personal struggles, which are almost definitely linked to your saboteurs.

WORRY IS A WASTE OF TIME

SELF-AWARENESS

WORRY IS DEBILITATING.
I discovered that the best thing I can do is put all that energy spent on worry into focusing on changing the situation. Worry won't change the situation—but actions will. Practically speaking, as we move into a decade of heightened uncertainty, our worry levels will tend to increase. Yet worrying won't solve the challenges we face.

Try this experiment. Take a holiday from worry for a month. Focus on action or on simply feeling excited about the future you want to create for yourself. *Excitement is a powerful form of intention, and intention becomes action quite naturally.*

YOUR HOME-PLAY

Now take a holiday from worry. Put any and all fears on the shelf for 30 days and let yourself not worry about a thing. If the worry pops up, put it aside and tell it "Later, mate!" Tell yourself you'll think about it once the 30 days are up, but not before.

If 30 days feels too long, begin with a day. Then build up to a week. Then a month.

Write down the top 10 things that you are worried about right now:

1.

2.

3.

4.

5.

6.

7.

8.

9.

10.

Todays date: _ _ _ / _ _ _ / _ _ _   30 days away:_ _ _ _ / _ _ _ / _ _ _

At the end of 30 days, come back to the worries you wrote down. How many of the things you were worried about have somehow become less worrisome after being starved of all the oxygen you were giving them?

After your holiday from worrying, write your results here.

How did you do? Were you able to stop worrying? Cross-check your top 10 list of worries.

Did any worries disappear for good or diminish considerably?

Have you changed your thinking on something that was consuming you before your holiday?

#6

LET PEOPLE BE DICKS SOMETIMES

EXTERNAL INFLUENCE

EVERY ONE OF US has been a dick at some point or another. Dickishness is when we act out of character, when we're a bit crabbier or a touch more self-centered, or even when we do or say hurtful things to get a rise.

Let's give each other the benefit of the doubt. This is how we make room for grace to enter the equation. When we don't give the benefit of the doubt, we lock people into being their worst selves, even if it was just momentary. In that moment, we don't allow each other to grow and evolve from whatever pain is causing us to act out. It's a lose-lose for everyone involved.

Let's not turn our backs and leave momentarily dickish people in that space! Changing the world for the better starts with the simple step of helping people emerge from a tough moment to become their best selves.

GIVE THEM SOME LOVE

List out uncharacteristic dickish behavior you've seen in people in your community lately and make an appointment to speak (gently) with those people.

What dickish behavior—temporary or perhaps even sustained—do you recognize in yourself?

#8

INTEGRITY AND VALUES

SELF-EMPOWERMENT

INTEGRITY ACCORDING TO the *Cambridge Dictionary*, it is "the quality of being honest and having strong moral principles that you refuse to change."

I'll define the three qualities that stand out to me in someone who strikes me as living with integrity: they know who they are, they commit to their word, and they always speak the truth. Living with integrity means having deep clarity about your personal values.

One of life's gifts is that you get to pick *your* values. When you're sure what they are, they light a guiding path ahead for you. They make decisions simpler. Does it fit? Or not? How can whatever it is be adjusted so that it aligns with your values?

They'll lead you through whatever you do for the rest of your life.

INTEGRITY IN ACTION

Who in your life is someone you consider a person of deep integrity? What are the qualities they have that you respect?

Do you see yourself as a person of integrity? Describe where you see yourself as really acting in alignment with your values.

Has life made you slip a bit or compromise on your values in some way? Can you determine what or who did that to you? Where have you slipped up? Which values do you feel you've let yourself down on?

What are your foundational personal values? Identify them, work out what they are, define what's important. List them here.

AIM PAST THE TOP OF THE HILL

SELF-EMPOWERMENT

IN LIFE, NOT MANY OF US even aim for the top—most people quit before they get there. But it's not even about the top, it's about getting past the top.

This became a guiding metaphor in my life: aim past the top of the hill. That's where real glory resides.

REFLECTIONS

What is my metaphorical hill?

When have I given up? Even before I hit the top, let alone over the top of the hill?

What does aiming past the top of the hill look like for me? What could I achieve if I did this?

What three things am I going to do differently to focus on getting over the hill, not just to the top of it?

1.

2.

3.

CONTROL YOUR OWN NARRATIVE

CAREER THOUGHTS

CONTROLLING YOUR OWN NARRATIVE is fundamentally about not getting lost in someone else's story—be it your husband, wife, friend, or anyone else. This is a path society tends to tell us to take. And then one day, finding ourselves alone, we don't know our own story because we haven't been the one telling it. We've been a supporting actor all along in another person's story.

Think of this as writing a happy ending into your narrative.

WRITE YOUR OWN STORY

Step 1: If your partner left today, are you in a position to move forward? Or would it cripple you financially?

Step 2: If it would cripple you, what commitments are you going to make to get something back for yourself? Think study, work, volunteering, gaining new skills, etc.

Step 3: What is the first commitment you're going to get cracking on?

Step 4: Are you telling yourself you're not good enough, not worthy, useless, more? Read *#Do you have voices in your head? (wisdom 4)* and get moving forward.

Notice the actions you take as you put this narrative into action.

Please, just don't leave yourself in a position to be stranded. It happens too often. Keep something for yourself, always.

#12

FROM
JUDGMENT TO
COMPASSION

SELF-AWARENESS

BEING COMPASSIONATE TOWARDS our fellow humans doesn't justify bad behavior. It doesn't absolve people from accountability. It simply helps you adjust your perspective—away from judgment, which doesn't help anyone, and toward compassion, which creates the space for change, action, and evolution.

None of us are perfect. We can all look deeper and ask better questions. So, let's be more compassionate and help people out of challenges. Let's lift each other up and create a better world for all of us.

When we help our neighbors, everyone in our community thrives.

HAVE A THINK

Who around you do you find yourself judging? How can you look at them from a viewpoint of compassion instead?

What can you do to help foster compassion rather than judgement in your community?

#13

MY RECIPE FOR TRUE LOVE

SELF-EMPOWERMENT

DON'T BE SCARED OF LOVE. If you can let go of the fear of getting hurt, rejected, or ridiculed and give yourself permission to pour yourself fully into love, it's amazing when it happens. If you've ever seen a couple that embodies your idea of true love, you know it's possible, and it shouldn't be as rare as it is.

While you bide your time, don't let anyone tell you you're being too fussy. People said that to me all the time. If you've decided to be fussy about the person that's going to be by your side for life, that's nobody's business but your own! Love is worth daydreaming for, and it's definitely worth waiting for.

CAPTURE YOUR DREAM

What does your dream person look like?

What's important to them?

What are the important values they must have?

How about work ethic or any preference for type of work? Free and wild, or serious and stable?

Want to have children, or want to live life adventuring?

How do you want them to feel about you?

These questions are just a start. Answers these or create your own. Write it down. Make a vision board.[1] Draw, write a poem, paint a picture—however you like to capture ideas.

Just spend some time thinking deeply about who you want by your side, then daydream about it every chance you get.

And if it works—if that vision turns into a reality—make sure you drop me a note on social media to tell me. I'll be so excited for you. Love is beautiful and worth focusing on to get the right match for you. Good luck and believe. You can be one of those inspiring couples who show the world that true love is real. xxxx

1   For vision board ideas, take a look at https://www.developgoodhabits.com/vision-board-ideas/

#14

FIND YOUR PURPOSE

SOCIAL LEADERSHIP

PURPOSE IS AS UNIQUE as each of us. Identifying it can transform your life.

So, what is *your* purpose? Purpose is not a brain decision, it's a heart decision. It may be as simple as the action that drives you and makes you want to get out of bed in the morning, with a spring in your step and purpose beating from your soul. Or is it something bigger, more ambitious? Size it right for you.

Is it more than one thing? You're not required to laser-focus on just one purpose in life!

Remember to be careful, though; not everyone is well-positioned to advise you and it's really important you don't speak with people who will make you feel or think smaller. Always be very selective in your advisers.

It's a joy to be driven this way, even if your purpose is challenging. You're doing it. That's a special life and a legacy to leave behind.

QUESTIONS TO PONDER

Are you open to your life having a purpose (or two or three)? Equally, is this life about a rest or a challenge? There is no wrong or right in this answer.

If you do want to define your purpose, who do you trust to explore this with? Who will expand you in this?

What are the things that are special about you? What excites you? What are the words that describe you and the things you care about?

What do you get really passionate about? Or even angry or outraged about? Hint, hint: this is always a sign of what is meaningful to you.

#18

EXUDE LOVE

SELF-EMPOWERMENT

THIS WISDOM IS LESS AN ACTION and more a state of being: exude love in everything you do and in everything that you are. It's a life-changer, I promise.

When we're in the energy of love, we are more at peace and more forgiving. We are more compassionate, with our eyes wider open.

At the start, try this experiment in the morning, on a day when you wake up and feel a skip in your step. Start small. Practice small for big, lasting results.

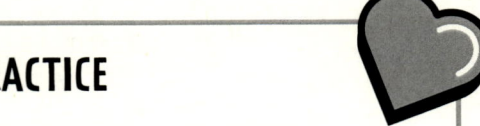

PRACTICE

Step 1: Close your eyes, calm your breathing, and focus on your heart.

Step 2: Imagine beautiful white light sitting in and all around your heart.

Step 3: Once you can "see" that light, take hold of it and push it through your body. Feel it flowing through you, feel it living in you, and feel the peace it brings you.

Step 4: Practice holding onto that feeling in your body when you come out of this micro-meditation and for as long as you can, project it into how you speak and act and your attitude towards others.

Give it a try. To build your white-light love muscle, practice. Even what feels like a tiny flicker will make a difference.

#19

IT'S TIME TO HONOR MOTHER EARTH

CLIMATE COURAGE

AT SOME LEVEL, all of us are responsible for this. Finding solutions will require courage and global commitment. It also requires simple individual steps, starting now.

Step 1 is to face it. It's time to recognize our behavior for what it is—and stop. It's like choosing to get healthy. Change is achieved one day at a time, and it helps a lot to have a clear goal of how you'll look and feel once you get there.

Step 2 is to decide to get healthy by changing our lifestyles. Each of us can make small deliberate changes in our lifestyle that are healthy for Mother Earth.

Step 3 is to realize that each of us counts. Your actions count. It is time to write a new future for all life on earth. We have the opportunity to do it right now.

WHAT CAN WE DO?

- Understand the scale of the situation. I share a Weekend Reads blog every week on andreatedwards.com, and it starts with climate news.

- Own your own contribution to the climate crisis. Change your lifestyle to reduce your footprint. Pick one area to address each month. In 12 months, your little bits add up to a lot!

- Share knowledge to awaken your community and help them see a course of action.

- If you work for a company, push for it to be emissions-neutral or negative within the shortest timeframe possible—by 2025 or 2030, for example. Later than this is simply too late.

- Vote for leaders who will do all they can to tackle the climate crisis.

- Show up—online to build momentum and in person for protests and action groups.

- Do not buy from companies continuing to abuse the environment. Name and shame the ones who are.

Notes: what actions am I committed too — list it out

1. _____

2. _____

3. _____

4. _____

5. _____

SCAN ME

TRUST
YOUR OWN
COUNSEL

CAREER THOUGHTS

NOT EVERYBODY IS IN A POSITION to give you meaningful advice. Why would they? Everyone comes at life from very different perspectives, experiences, and expectations.

Which is why trusting your own counsel is a strength, not a weakness or an arrogance. You take input and advice from those around you and then you draw your own conclusions, based on your knowledge, your experience, and your insights.

INTO ACTION

Am I strong in trusting my own counsel?

When have I taken advice that was not aligned with my own counsel?

Why did I listen to this advice? (Think deeply on that.)

Did I do something differently in life or work because I did listen?

Is it too late to change direction, back into alignment with my own counsel?
(Hint, it's never too late.)

What kind of advice am I seeking right now?

Who is aligned to me and can help me on my way?

If I were a friend coming to me for advice, how would I advise myself?

#22

WHAT YOU RESIST PERSISTS

SELF-AWARENESS

IF YOU'RE FEELING STUCK in what you're doing and unhappy with where you are, but you know where you want to be, work really hard not to wallow in the energy of hating where you are. That's resistance.

Instead, move into the energy of taking yourself where you want to go—in your mind and in the actions you take.

Some simple ways to identify resistance: When you hear yourself saying words like: "Why me?" or, "This isn't fair!" or, "It wasn't meant to be this way!"

When you attempt to control something that is out of your hands, it often extends your suffering. Resistance is a refusal to accepting what is right in front of our noses.

The truth is, you don't have to like it, but once you accept it—even without joy in your hearts—your suffering lessens or goes away.

Instead, put that energy and your empowered selves into action for the change you want.

HOMEWORK

Apply it to yourself:

What are you resisting in your life? Work, marriage, kids, anything? List it out, then ask yourself: can I give myself a week or a month off resisting any or all of this so I can test this idea out?

If you can't think of anything, consider anything that makes you miserable. Anything that doesn't bring you joy. Any relationship dynamic that has been constantly negative for some time, a behavior in someone else that you just can't tolerate? We all resist something, and when we let the resistance go—really go—it regularly disappears. We sometimes must give it more time, if it is a long-term issue.

Check in one week/month later. Did anything go away while you weren't resisting it?

SELF-EMPOWERMENT

FOR ME, *trust first* was something I had to learn.

Trust first might feel like a dramatic shift for you, but it's what we naturally did as kids. Give it a try when you're meeting somebody new. Go in with an open heart and you're likely to be met with the same in return.

Open that connection and see if it's something to build on. If it doesn't work out, move on—don't get stuck in it

A trust-first mentality is not foolishness or gullibility. It allows people to enter your life fully as themselves. When you drop your guard or stages to earning trust, you get to the core faster and build more amazing relationships faster too. Welcome strangers. The vast majority of them will be awesome.

I _____

Promise to be **open**
to NEW PEOPLE entering my Life.

I won't make them pass a TEST of TRUST
I will welcome them with **OPEN ARMS**

If they show me they are not
trustworthy, I will let
them go gently, and not take it on
board as any sort of FAILING.
They are NOT RIGHT FOR ME.

That is OK.

And for every person I meet who I
know is not right for me, it will NOT
make me bitter & closed off to the NEXT.

I will stay open to WONDER

_____
SIGNED

TIM HAMONS

51

#25

IT'S OK TO WALK AWAY

SELF-EMPOWERMENT

HAVE YOU STUCK WITH a passion even after the passion has died? I did, and it was awful.

REFLECTION

Where in your life might there be something you need to walk away from?

An activity?

A friendship or business relationship?

A romantic relationship?

Which is it? Any?

What is stopping you from walking away?

What action will you take that respects you, those involved and your future?

#26

EPIPHANIES
ON ANGER

SELF-AWARENESS

ONE OF THE GREATEST LESSONS I've learned in life is about letting go of anger. This does not mean I don't get angry—it means anger doesn't control me.

Neale Donald Walsch once said, *"Anger expressed is never about the person it's directed towards. It's always about the person who is angry."* I heard this wise man's words at the right time; they went in deep and forced me to reflect. Catching and questioning yourself when you feel angry needs to be a continual and conscious practice. It will help you dig deep into your self-awareness and understand where the anger is really coming from. And it will improve and make more joyous your relationships with the people you tend to project that anger onto.

The important thing is, any time you feel anger, go inside and ask: is it them? Or is it me? The latter will be your answer most of the time, if you can be fully honest with yourself. Acknowledging this changed my life, and I hope it changes yours.

REFLECTION

What are your frustrations with someone or something in your life? Think deep and list it down, all of it. Be completely honest with yourself—what's getting your goat?

Take a minute or two to go within and work out what it is that you are projecting onto others in your life.

Every time you can, when you feel anger rise in you, stop, think, reflect and ask yourself: am I angry towards them, or is it something deeper? This is a wonderful muscle to develop.

#28

THE ONE-MINUTE MEDITATION

SOCIAL LEADERSHIP

I DEVELOPED THIS ONE-MINUTE meditation for my executive clients at IBM, BNP Paribas Securities Services, DHL, Microsoft, and beyond. I use it to help clients define their core focus as social leaders.

One thing I've observed when working with executive teams is that they're often so busy in their minds they can't connect easily with the wisdom in their hearts. I put this meditation together as a fast way to tap into the subconscious mind. For anyone who feels this all sounds a bit *woo-woo*, you should let the fact that it has worked spectacularly well with business executives alleviate any reluctance you might have towards giving it a go. It won't harm you, I promise! And it might just do you a world of good.

Be open. Give it a go and see what comes up.

CONTEXT

To gain clarity on your focus or life goals, it is important to reflect and consider what you want to be known for, or what you want to do with your life.

The following meditation will hopefully help you, if you approach it with an open mind and look at it as a starting point for the journey to becoming your whole, best, beautiful self.

THE INSTRUCTIONS

1. Sit down with paper and pen, your phone, or a computer—or simply use the space below in this book. The important thing is to have everything you need to write ready in front of you before you start. Clear away unnecessary clutter.

2. Read the questions below. Select one that speaks to you *right now*. All of these questions are relevant. You can go back and do the others separately later.

3. Get comfortable in a quiet place where you won't be disturbed. Uncross your arms and legs and set your timer for one minute plus 10 seconds. (Those extra 10 seconds will give you time to relax.)

4. Start your timer, close your eyes, take some deep breaths, and relax.

5. When you're ready, silently ask yourself the question you chose— over and over again—until the alarm goes off. Push away any other thoughts that attempt to break in while you're doing this exercise. Just keep asking your question over and over again, meditating on it for one minute.

6. When the timer goes off, open your eyes and start writing. Write whatever comes up, and if nothing comes up, doodle or scribble. Do not judge what is coming out, just write for as long as you need to write and capture the messages that emerge from your subconscious.

In front of you will be words, sentences, paragraphs, or maybe even patterns. Consider your words. Do you have your answers there? Are you surprised by what you see? Or are these the words you knew would come?

If you are struggling or apprehensive about doing this, invite a good friend or colleague to do this exercise with you. When you get your results, you can discuss it together. Regardless, the answer to your question is here. Be open to seeing it.

MEDITATION QUESTIONS

Reminder: all questions are equal, so select the one that speaks to you today.

- What do I want to do with my life?

- What do I want to be known for?

- What makes me stand out in a crowd?

- When I light people up, what is it I am talking about?

- What is my expertise?

- What am I unique at?

- What are my core values?

- What comes easily to me?

- What do I read about until the early hours of the morning?

- What gets me out of bed eagerly?

- What gives me energy?

- What feeds my spirit?

- What do people compliment me on?

- What makes me amazing?

NOTES AND INSIGHTS

Now spend some time defining your message and make a plan to contribute your voice to the world. And for insights on how you can be a social leader, follow my blogs on **andreatedwards.com**.

DON'T BE A MAYBE

EMPOWER OTHERS

REMEMBER THE DAYS when your RSVP to an event or a party meant a simple *yes or no*? There were two possible responses. You committed, one way or the other.

These days, we've moved into a world where there's a third box: Maybe. It's not good.

SIGN THE PLEDGE

I promise not to be a *maybe*.

I promise to honor the people organizing events and social gatherings. I'll be clear on my *yes* and my *no* and show up when I've promised to.*

_____

Signed

_ _ _ / _ _ _ / _ _ _

Dated

*This is powerful wisdom that applies well beyond your social life.

SEIZE YOUR MOMENTS

SELF-EMPOWERMENT

ALL THROUGHOUT OUR LIVES, we are given moments to shine. If we seize them and excel, doors open up to more of what we want in life. We find our feet on unexpected paths.

Have you seized your moments?

Or did you panic and fail?

The secret to achieving what we really want is about seizing these moments when they arise throughout the course of our lives. There will be many of them.

Recognizing them is the key, and then having the courage to step up and rise to the challenge we've set for ourselves. Should we fail, we keep at it, again and again and again, learning a bit each time until we succeed.

HOME-PLAY

What were the moments I seized?

What were the moments I didn't seize?

What were the reasons I didn't seize my moment/s?

What can I do right now to seize the future I want for myself? Where can I step it up?

Who around me has amazing potential that needs support to seize *their* moment?

WATCH OUT FOR NEGATIVE NELLIES

EXTERNAL INFLUENCE

IS THERE ANYTHING MORE DRAINING than spending time with people who are constantly negative?

Now, I get it that crap stuff happens in life. But my life experiment has taught me this: wallowing in negativity consumes your soul. It makes your spirit stingy. It drains the person being negative, and it also drains everyone around them.

Watching out for the negative Nellies is really about watching out for this habit in ourselves—the habit of holding onto something negative to get attention. It's a habit you can break if you see it in yourself.

It requires a mindset shift grounded in action. That action is a daily check-in to keep any negative tendencies down. When you feel the urge to complain or to say negative things, *even if those negative things are hilarious and will garner laughs and likes on social media*, check yourself and ask whether it would honestly change anything for the better? Nine times out of ten, the answer will be no.

When you do your daily check-in, focus on the increase in the positive things you see and experience.

And as for those people in your life who wallow in negativity, you can help them too, and break the cycle by giving them positive support (see **#Breath in Love, breath out hate**, *wisdom 47*).

HELPING OTHERS

If you know someone who is a negative Nellie and it's becoming harder and harder to spend time with them, but you still care about them, try one or all of these:

1. Speak to them about their negativity and how it makes you feel when you're around them.

2. Take them on an adventure—somewhere quirky, with life in abundance—and ask them to share the most amazing experiences they're having as they're having it, as well as the craziest stuff they're seeing. Make it a day for taking the best photograph and share those together at the end (and on social media if that's where they do most of their negative wallowing). Check in on them a few days afterwards. See if they're still buzzing from the experience together, and put another outing on the calendar. Keep the momentum up and give them something to look forward to.

3. Take them to a place where life is really hard and show them your compassion in action for the people you meet. Ask those people to tell you their stories.

4. Help them understand how to watch their thoughts and flip them when negative reactions arise.

5. Write in permanent ink, on their bathroom mirror, how awesome they are.

6. Leave them loving notes, send small gifts to make them smile, show them they are thought of and loved. If social media is where they do their negative wallowing, engage with them positively there. This can take an amazing amount of negative wind out of their sails!

ACTIONS

1. Who do you care about that is being a Negative Nellie?

2. What will you do to help them? Pick one of these or come up with some-thig special of your own.

3. When are you going to do it?

And tick it off when you do!

CAREER THOUGHTS

ONE DAY WHEN I WAS FOUR, my dad put me in front of the TV and said, "Watch this." It was "Bohemian Rhapsody," and that was the start of my love affair with Queen and Freddie Mercury. I've learned a lot from Freddie.

- **Freddie broke ALL the rules.**
  (To paraphrase one of my favorite Seth Godin quotes: if we follow the data, all we get is more of the Kardashians. Same goes for rules.)

- **Freddie had an unbreakable belief in himself!**

- **Freddie owned his genius.**

- **Freddie wasn't looking for shortcuts to success.**

- **Freddie embraced his showmanship.**

- **Freddie understood his audience.**

QUEENLY REFLECTIONS

Who's your hero/ine and why?

What qualities do they have that you admire?

Which of those qualities could you focus on developing?

What rules do you play by that need to be broken?

#35

BEWARE THE VICTIM MINDSET

SELF-AWARENESS

WHEN THINGS AREN'T GOING WELL, it's easy to blame the company you're working for or the people in your life. In a relationship, it's very easy to blame the rough times on your partner. If you can't get on top of everything as a parent, it's easy to blame the children.

But in reality, the only way we can ever overcome challenges is to face into them and take responsibility for them ourselves. Recognizing and reversing a victim mindset requires a deep level of self-awareness.

Getting out of a victim mindset is critical to putting yourself in control of how your life turns out. When you stop being a victim, it empowers you. Focus on the words you use. Focus on how they disempower you, not excuse you from being and achieving what you wish in life.

Step 1 is to assume responsibility for having a victim mindset.

Step 2 is to pounce on these thoughts immediately. This can be hard (see **#Do you have voices in your head?**, *wisdom 4*).

Step 3 is to look at where there is a problem in your life, a problem where you are the common denominator. Reflect on your role and on what you need to take ownership of and what you can change.

Personal responsibility is well within your reach—and it's powerful.

PUT IT INTO ACTION

Do I have a victim mindset? (If you're not sure, run through the questions in the text in the book to see if any of them sound like something you say, either to yourself or out loud.)

Is it just sometimes, or am I really bad?

What are the challenges that keep showing up in my life that I haven't been taking responsibility for?

What am I going to do about changing them? List three commitments!

1.

2.

3.

GIVERS AND TAKERS

EXTERNAL INFLUENCE

WHEN YOU'RE NOT NATURALLY a taker, it can be confusing to encounter those who just don't understand that life is as much about the give as the take—especially if you want to have a fulfilling and beautiful experience in this world. And if you are constantly giving to someone who always puts themselves first and always takes, it can definitely be exhausting.

When a taker takes too much, and you've already given all you have to give, step away graciously, gently to get on with doing you. Protect yourself, move forward, and be careful about welcoming more takers into your life. Be generous but not at your own expense. (**#Self-protection and the circle of trust**, *wisdom 68*)

If a taker asks you why you stopped giving, keep in mind that tough love is a favor you may choose to give them, but sometimes it can make the situation worse.

You have to make a decision based on who you know this person to be.

But the critical lesson I've learned for ensuring you don't diminish your own light (and beauty) is to not let takers change your generous spirit. Even if you can't change them, do not let them change you.

COLLECT YOUR THOUGHTS

Who are the takers in my life? Can I help them? Do I have the energy to spare for that?

What about my role in this?

What am I giving to someone who always takes?

Why do I do it?

What is in me that feels the need to give to someone who always leaves me a little let down?

Is it time to address this within myself

Am I seeking some form of validation from them?

If I agree to help the takers, what three things will I do for them?

1.

2.

3.

HAVE YOU MET YOUR SOUL YET?

SELF-EMPOWERMENT

I HAVE A CLASSIC MONKEY MIND. It bounces around and it's always on. It's curious and it'll try anything. It is open to anything.

So, when it was suggested that I try a guided meditation to get to know myself better, I didn't think much would come of it. A monkey mind and meditation had never been a great match for me, but I was game to try.

In doing so, I gained a deeper sense of who I am.

Since that first time, I have meditated many times. Here is one that I always come out feeling amazing.

I call this meditation *Have you met your soul yet?*

(You may also enjoy **#The one-minute meditation**, *wisdom 28*)

SOUL EXPLORATION

Sit back and relax. Imagine or meditate if you can. What is the highest version of you?

What qualities and values do you have in this version of yourself? I find guided meditation—even self-guided—unbelievably powerful to get to these answers.

What are your best qualities? Your most beautiful essence? Do you know it?

Some people find drawing to be a useful tool to tap into this part of who they are. What symbols would represent this highest version of yourself?

Are you struggling to answer this? Find a meditation practitioner where you live and ask them to help you take this journey! Show them the chapter and see if they are open to helping you achieve this.

#38

FORGIVENESS IS FOR YOU

SELF-EMPOWERMENT

IF YOU'VE LIVED, you have likely been wronged. You may still be in pain from it.

When we don't forgive, we allow those who've wronged us to live and linger in our bodies, minds, and hearts—poisoning us, sickening us, and worsening our lives.

When the wrong was unintentional, which it often is, they often have no idea we even feel that way. However serious the wound, it's our story, not theirs, and in order to heal we need to be conscious of the fact that we control that story.

When you forgive, you let go of this story and release its toxins. If you don't, it eats away at you.

So, what are the practical steps to take toward forgiveness, which is definitely easier said than done?

This is what I do.

BOLTS OF FORGIVENESS

Step 1: Notice when you feel negative feelings towards someone who you think has done you wrong.

Step 2: Close your eyes and picture a huge ball of clean, love-based light, sitting in your heart.

Step 3: Then use all of your energy to throw this bolt of white light from your heart and aim it straight at the heart of the person you're angry with.

Do this anytime a negative, sad, or angry thought comes up.

Don't do this for them. Do it for you. Forgiveness is always for you and your own good. Let go of your hate and move on from that story, because it's time for the next chapter of your life to commence.

MY COMMITMENT

I will send daily bolts of white light to:

WHAT IS SUFFERING FOR?

SELF-AWARENESS

PEOPLE SUFFERING DEVELOP a mindset of suffering that does not end when the traumatic incident or period might come to an end, for the human body encodes trauma into its tissue. Suffering becomes integrated into our lives.

I've learned to look at suffering in terms of what we can gain or learn through it. It can teach us strength, passion, purpose, and beauty. That is where we've really gotten the concept of suffering wrong. It is a gift of growth, and a challenge to be overcome, but it is not a place to reside, a state of being to accept as an inevitable test of faith.

When it consumes us and prevents our joy, that's when it's time to stop accepting suffering, time to buck against it.

And for each of us personally, when we suffer—as we have all suffered during this pandemic—can we emerge from it kinder, more beautiful, more community-minded?

PRACTICE

Ask yourself: am I suffering?

Have you uncovered any growth, learning, or opportunities through our collective suffering in this pandemic experience?

Do you believe you have the right to claim suffering, when so many others are suffering more? Many of us struggle with this, the notion that our own pain is not worthy of being called suffering. However, when we do not fully acknowledge and validate our own feelings, we cannot address them and move forward.

Are there any small steps that you can take to overcome this challenge? Some actions you can take right now which will reduce your current suffering? Whatever your answer, remember that it's OK to be in this moment with tears and pain. In order to move past our pain, we must first feel it.

More broadly, what can we do to help alleviate collective suffering?

Who can you see around you that might be suffering, and is there something immediate and tangible you can do?

Note: one of my dreams with this book is that some of you, dear readers, have the wisdom to take action for the millions of people suffering right now. What a gift it would be if we could make it happen. Let's come together and solve the world's biggest problems. No one should suffer starvation, desperation, and lack of dignity in a world of plenty.

#41

TAKE TIME OFF AND THINK

CAREER THOUGHTS

WHEN I CAN TRAVEL, even with two boys—or three if you count Steve—it's my quiet time, my thinking time. I use this time to go on adventures around this amazing world, which is pure soul food. But it's time I spend in my head, too, and it feeds my mind, my creativity, and my spirit. It allows me to put so many ideas into context with the larger world. My life and decisions can never be focused egocentrically when I live in this wider world.

The challenge is, we're just not giving ourselves the time for this melding of internal and external stimuli. In our busy daily world, we only hear the external, and that's a huge miss. Time for your own thoughts is too important not to rank at the top of your priorities.

Silence is a gift that will give you so much in return. Take it. Don't let life be a state of constant overwhelm or noise. Give yourself the time you need as you go through the process of a life redesign. There really has never been a better time.

MAKE A COMMITMENT

Your commitment to time off: what is it? When, where, how often, how long? Alone, with family, with spouse, with . . . ?

Determine one place to capture ideas—a notebook, app, etc. Put every idea in the same place.

Ideas you will marinate during your next time away: list ones that have been hanging around, unresolved for a while. Come back to this if the epiphanies don't strike immediately, but do make an effort to actively capture the thoughts when they arise.

1.

2.

3.

4.

5.

6.

7.

8.

9.

10.

PRO TIP: for a beautiful shortcut to capture ideas, download Otter.ai. Speak into the app and it will transcribe your thoughts.

#43

THE BEAUTY OF ABUNDANT THINKING

SELF-EMPOWERMENT

INTUITIVELY, MANY OF US UNDERSTAND that what we think defines and shapes our lives. When I understood the idea of what an *abundance mindset* really meant, I decided to throw myself into an experiment at a time we were on our knees, financially. When the chips were down, I decided to put abundant thinking to the test.

But there is an underlying message beyond mere selfish acquisitions in abundant thinking that speaks to me powerfully.

When you think about how our thoughts control our reality, then surely, when we speak about money only with words of *lack*, that's going to lead to more lack. Furthermore, why should abundant thinking only apply to financial outcomes?

All of this was going on in the background as I fully threw myself into my abundance experiment on every level.

No lack thinking was allowed in my life. I was vigilant about my mindset, my family, my work, my contribution to my colleagues, and how I made other people in my community feel.

What I found was that the more I leaned into the abundance experiment, the more energy I allowed to flow *through* me—energy of plenty, peace, and hope—the more I received in return, in terms of financial success, community, love.

Abundant thinking is recognizing that there's enough and that you're OK as you are. When you are OK as you are, you don't crave more because you are already abundant.

From a logical level, this is a really hard concept to embrace. You have to completely surrender to the idea. If you can fully surrender and live *in* an abundance mindset, your life will transform.

When you have this mindset, the people around you feel it and they too feel energized by your vibe. They want to be part of it. They want in. It's beautiful. Embrace it.

GETTING ABUNDANT

Step 1: Identify one area in your life that feels constrained of lacking.

Step 2: Think about it from a "there is enough" mindset.

Step 3: And surrender to it. Really surrender 100%!

For example: Say you're not getting enough recognition. Change it to "I have enough recognition" and see how you change. Because it's always about you, not the external environment. This, for me, is what an abundance mindset is about.

Be open to what happens. Who knows where it will take you? That's the beauty, but one thing for sure, it will take you to a better place, not worse.

And yes, you can repeat this more than once on the same area before moving to another area of your life.

Right now, with the whole world locked in struggle, it is a great time to try the experiment. What have you got to lose? And the good news about abundance is that it's abundant!

JOIN THE GIVING ECONOMY

SOCIAL LEADERSHIP

THE GIVING ECONOMY VALUES generosity ahead of money. It helps each of us be more for each other, as communities and as friends, it's so much more than a dollar sign.

On social media, the giving economy is actually easy. Comment on and share other's ideas. Be a champion for your community.

Is someone you admire running a workshop or a public event? Share it. If you love creative people—musicians, artists, performers—go out of your way to support and promote what they do. Do you have friends fighting for the environment or social justice? Be their biggest cheerleader and you'll be contributing to those movements, too.

We fall over ourselves to interact with and *like* famous people online. Let's do the same for those people closest to us. They need it. Participation and engagement in your immediate network will make it stronger and more vibrant for everyone.

WHICH ONES OF THESE ARE YOU GOING TO COMMIT TO ON SOCIAL MEDIA?

BREATH IN LOVE, BREATH OUT HATE

SELF-EMPOWERMENT

IF YOU'VE EVER DONE MEDITATION, mindfulness, yoga, or anything similar, there's a strong chance you've been asked to breath in love and breath out hate—or a variation on this—as part of the practice.

This is a surprisingly effective exercise. Anytime you feel deep anger, just do this exercise for a few seconds and see if you can let go. It's worth getting past the first bit of discomfort to feel these words deeply, powerfully.

Breath in love, breath out hate. Breath in love, breath out hate. Breath in love, breath out hate. Breath in love, breath out hate.

ACTION

Do this for a minute . . . for yourself: *Breath in love, breath out hate.*

And if you know of someone who needs it . . . plant some karma points and do this exercise while thinking of them. Share it with them if you think they'd be open.

If you are feeling a general sense of unease, sadness, frustration, loneliness, or whatever else may be happening for you right now, just do this a couple of times a day. One minute each time. It will help you feel better, promise.

#49

IT'S TIME TO SPEAK UP

SOCIAL LEADERSHIP

ARE YOU READY TO STAND UP for what you believe in? Yes? Then now is the time to put your big girl/big boy pants on and do it. If you believe it is time to change the path for humanity and all life on earth, now is our chance to make it happen. If you want to see a kinder, more generous, more loving and equal world, now is the time to claim it.

When we speak up, we drive the global conversation back into alignment with how the majority of us are feeling. Striving for such balance is critical right now! We cannot allow the negative and depressing narrative to continue to consume us. We can't stop extremists speaking up. But we are bigger, and we can take responsibility by showing up.

HOW DO YOU SHOW UP EFFECTIVELY?

Step 1: Define the message you want to be known for. (**#Find your voice**, wisdom 17)

Step 2: Connect deeply to your own intentions. Sit in the energy of purpose to envision the change you're seeking to drive, the awareness you're seeking to build. If you can connect on that deepest level, it's incredibly fortifying. (**#The one-minute meditation**, wisdom 28)

Step 3: From this position, grow your voice, your influence, and your power to create a better future for humanity and all life on earth. Anchor your presence deeply in your intentions and go!

If you want to polish up your social presence online, there is plenty of help out there. For starters, check out my website where I blog on this topic extensively.

GET OUTSIDE
YOUR SUCCESS
ECHO CHAMBER

CAREER THOUGHTS

HAVE YOU EVER BEEN TOLD to only spend time with people you admire and aspire to be like, to ensure you are successful like them? I certainly have.

What qualities do you really want to aspire to, and therefore, who do you really need to be around?

If you want to be successful, hang out with successful people for sure, but first answer the question: what does *success* mean to you? When you've defined success, find the people who model it for you, and also find the people who define success differently, especially in your society or culture.

The important thing is to watch and reflect on what *you* want—not what others want for you.

With all of humanity to learn from, cast your net wide and be in dialogue with people whose ideas or ways of thinking are fundamentally different to yours.

HOME-PLAY

List the people you are going to speak to about their definition of success:

List the various experiences and backgrounds you will seek to learn from—through your reading, writing, watching, etc.

#51

THERE IS ENOUGH TO GO AROUND

SELF-EMPOWERMENT

ONE OF THE THINGS I LEARNED in devoting myself to a truly abundant mindset was that judgment, envy, and cynicism cannot co-exist with abundance. Let's just say the chemical reaction between the three of them forms an abundance-blocking compound in us.

Identify where you express—in thoughts or words—judgment, envy, and/or cynicism. Be honest with yourself. Can you let it go? Can you release yourself from these negative thought patterns?

When you do, it's really easy to sink into the true energy of abundance. From there, you can watch your life become bigger, more beautiful, and yes, more abundant. Even in hard times, you can do this. I know you can, because I've been there, too.

CHECK-IN

Have any of your thoughts or actions in the last day come from judgment, envy, and cynicism? List it out!

It is incredibly easy to sink into these negative mindsets, especially at moments when life is particularly tough. The important thing is to watch your thoughts carefully, and if something negative comes up, pull yourself up instantly and halt it. Then put that attention toward a constructive view of the world that fits your values.

Even simpler: if you have a moment of jealousy over someone else's achievement, catch yourself and switch to thinking (or saying), "Good on you mate, that's just fantastic!" Then get back to focusing on what you want to achieve, and keep working towards it, regardless. This mindset means you won't allow yourself to be distracted and pulled down by the energy that jealousy takes from you.

Build the muscle to stop yourself from doing this. It takes constant thought monitoring. Be vigilant if you want to stop doing it.

#52

POSITIVITY AIN'T ALL IT'S CRACKED UP TO BE

SELF-AWARENESS

WHILE NEGATIVITY AND CYNICISM are a poor foundation on which to build anything permanent, uncritical positivity is not the answer, either.

The truth is, my "negative" emotions are where I build my self-awareness muscles. I dig into them, I pick apart why I feel them, and then I release them. You can too.

Being positive is awesome. And being unflappable when things are terrible is even more awesome. It's about getting the balance right between the two, and it's about not being scared to face our negative emotions.

PRACTICE

Ask yourself: what's my balance between negative feelings and happy ones? On a scale of 0% (completely miserable and angry all the time) to 100% (a radiant saint), how would you rate yourself?

When something negative comes up in me, can I simply be OK with it while it plays itself out? Or do I fight it?

Do I accept that my negative emotions are something within me, or do I project them onto others?

How are my self-awareness muscles when it comes to facing up to my own negative emotions?

When I am angry, do I hold onto it for days, weeks, months or even years? Or am I able to release it quickly, after sinking into it?

My advice, spend a week trying to release anger quickly. You cannot release it if you continue to project it onto someone else, telling yourself it's their fault you feel this way. You can only release it when you accept it as your own emotion.

Blaming others and projecting is a HUGE part of the problem we all struggle with.

Think about why these negative emotions rise. What is it within yourself that you need to see? Frustration with yourself or your life, regrets, more?

Breath in and experience it, then breath it out. Biologically, many emotions last only up to 12 minutes—which is not so long!

REFUSE TO PLAY SMALL

SELF-AWARENESS

HEY, YOU—YEAH, YOU. Are you playing small in your life? Scared to put your head up for fear it will get chopped off? Worried what others will think of you? Anxious about losing the community around you? Scared of feeling foolish or ignored, of getting mocked, shamed, or laughed at?

You are not alone.

It's common to feel scared when we play a bigger game. But when we play small, we diminish our own potential, the gift we can give to the world. We diminish ourselves, constricting our voices and our legacy.

When we do this, we slip into a downward spiral in our lives, which could see us moving into our older years bitter and dissatisfied.

We risk regret, which is an ugly thing.

HAVE A THINK

Where are you playing small?

What have you always wanted to do but haven't?

What's held you back? Be honest and list it out.

What are you going to do now to play a bigger game?

What are your heart and mind calling you to do?

What first step will you take to get started?

#55

HOW TO DEAL WITH ECO-ANXIETY

CLIMATE COURAGE

MOVING PAST ECO-ANXIETY IS ESSENTIAL, once you've realized it's there. Once you get past these intense emotions, it's time for action.

SOME ACTIONS YOU CAN TAKE

Step 1: Start with yourself and your family. Look honestly at your lifestyle. Get ready to face up to the horror of how much you personally contribute to the mess. There are apps to help you calculate how much pollution you contribute, how much energy you use, and the impact of your flights. Take a look at the amount of plastic central to your lifestyle.

Step 2: Inventory your life top to bottom and pick some areas you will change.

Step 3: Make these changes. Maybe you'll buy less stuff (like clothes) or go the extra mile for sustainable solutions. Look for alternatives to the wasteful packaging and high carbon footprint of many supermarket products. Maybe you'll start composting, maybe you'll eat less meat. You may choose to use your mobile phone for longer instead of adding to the e-waste mountain. Maybe you'll choose to focus on making sure that everything that comes into your home is more efficient.

It's really about switching mindsets to create less waste in all aspects of life!

If it goes into the trash within minutes of buying it or getting it as a freebie, then it should never exist in the first place!

Step 4: Once you clean up your act, the next step is help promote awareness and get other people engaged.

It all adds up when each of us take action in different ways. We're all connected to different communities. You can speak up in the company you work for, or be at the coalface on the front line. You can be a spokesperson for your own community or nation, wherever you feel comfortable standing up.

WHERE ARE YOU ON THE ECO-ANXIETY SCALE?

ASK YOURSELF

How can I move to the next stage—beyond overwhelm and eco-anxiety—while being kind to myself? What is my first action to move past despair?

What's one commitment I can make this week that helps me become more climate positive?

Who is one person in my community I can speak with and encourage to join me on my climate positive journey?

Don't forget, share your journey and commitments with your community as you go. You might inspire others to join you!

#58

LEAD WITH COMPASSION

SELF-AWARENESS

IF YOU'VE COMMITTED TO BECOMING the best and kindest version of yourself, a critical aspect of the journey is discovering a deep well of compassion—towards others and yourself.

This compassion extends to those who've done you harm. It extends to people we don't even know.

Compassion is awareness of another's suffering and a desire to alleviate it.[2] We don't just observe the suffering—compassion means taking action to do something to change the situation.

It takes enormous courage and strength, especially if it is toward someone who hurt you. Compassion is a muscle we can exercise.

Compassion requires commitment.

2   https://blog.mindvalley.com/what-is-compassion/

PRACTICE

Is there someone in your life or community who has done you/yours great harm?

Who are they? What did they do?

What is their story? Early life, adult life? What happened to them? Who hurt them? When was the hurt?

Are they lost? Or do they have an opportunity for redemption?

Are you capable of helping, or is there someone else who should do it?

What communities and community support do you see available for those need-ing this kind of attention right now? If there isn't any, can you find other compassionate citizens and start building a community to help those in need?

GIVE YOURSELF PERMISSION TO DREAM

SELF-EMPOWERMENT

IT'S SO EASY TO GET SIDETRACKED from our dreams, whether due to social expectations, cultural pushback, or just too many people telling us why we can't do something. What's hard is to keep in mind is that they are expressing their own ideas and fears, and that those ideas and fears have absolutely nothing to do with us. (**#Trust your own counsel**, *wisdom 20*)

Stuff will happen. But, my friends, why not dream to be a superstar in your field if that's what you really, *really* want, deep down in your heart? Particularly if you're yearning for it daily.

You don't even have to tell anyone about your dream, just believe it deeply for yourself.

GET DREAMING

If those negative voices are still in your head, push them out for a bit (see **#Worry is a waste of time**, wisdom 5 and **#Do you have voices in your head?**, wisdom 4).

Get comfortable. Go to your happy place or for a walk out in nature. Listen to your heart.

What is your heart dreaming of?

What is your plan to start acting on that dream?

1.

2.

3.

4.

5.

The best way to move forward is to take that first step. Go and do it today. And if that voice in your head gives you an excuse, tell it to get lost and get going anyway.

#65

UNLEASH THE YEARNERS

EMPOWER OTHERS

DO YOU YEARN? Do you *allow* yourself to yearn? Please do! Yearning has three parts:

1. It is the starting point that creates desire

2. Desire turns into passion and determination

3. Determination gives you the wings and confidence to believe you can do anything!

You are free to yearn, and then you are free to act.

YEARNING IN ACTION

What do you yearn for?

Now give yourself permission to yearn and act! What will you do next?

Could you also take a moment or two to really feel for those who can never fully express it? What is it like for them? Is it fair that we continue building societies that suppress so many?

Then join the conversation to create real change around the world—a world of acceptance for all to be as they are. Are you in?

#68

SELF-PROTECTION AND THE CIRCLE OF TRUST

SELF-EMPOWERMENT

THE LONGER I LIVE, the clearer it is to me that the person most affected by my anger is *me*. Quite simply, I don't like the way anger feels in my body.

The circle of trust is a visual metaphor about self-protection and managing expectations. It's about not letting anger consume you.

THIS IS HOW TO WORK WITH THE CIRCLE OF TRUST

Step 1: When you first meet someone, they start with a huge bubble around them—in your mind. It's a circle that represents full trust.

Step 2: If they do something that's disloyal or selfish or shows they are incapable of being a great friend, that's fine; just shrink the circle and drop any expectations.

The circle metaphorically protects you. It keeps you out of harm's way by helping you readjust your expectations of people.

Step 3: Be compassionate. When you see them evolve, expand the circle. People change—they evolve, they grow. None of us are perfect.

We're all trying to do our best. These days, when I see someone really making an effort to evolve, their circle can grow again. It's a dynamic thing, a little gesture of faith in us all.

USING YOUR CIRCLE WISELY

Who needs their circle reduced? Be honest!

Whose could be expanded a bit (on reflection)?

Think of the key people in your life, the ones you are constantly fighting with, or with whom the relationship isn't adding to your happiness. What are the expectations you keep putting on them that they can't deliver on? Think deeply.

What do you want them to do differently that they are not doing? Can you remove the expectation and accept them as they are?

Give it a try and check in 30 days later. How has the relationship changed/improved?

You actively shrink your circle every time you remove expectations. They can't hurt you when you expect nothing from them.

SELF-AWARENESS

EVERYONE DESERVES RESPECT.

In my 30 years of travel, I've seen so many examples of people speaking badly to those they consider *beneath* them, while they speak nicely and respectfully to those they see as being their equals or superiors.

Often, the deference and respect are for something on the surface: skin tone, religion, nationality, perceived social status, etc.

If I could rid the world of one thing right now, it is this idea that some people are naturally superior and that the others are inferior.

Kindness is meaningless when it's not given equally. No one is above you and no one is beneath you.

Be kind to everyone and watch life blossom.

PRACTICE

Have you been known to speak badly to people in your life? Whether it's people in your community, a different race or culture? Servants? Darker skinned people?

Do you come from a culture where these hierarchical layers are normal? And if so, are you aware of your participation in maintaining this status quo?

Or is this something you've never thought about? I appreciate that this is very often the case. But perpetuating these ideas doesn't serve us or make our community—and ultimately the world—a better place.

Do you think you *are* superior to certain people? Who and why?

Make a commitment now. Next time you feel yourself wanting to snap at someone or criticize them, take a breath and shift your words (and heart) to something kind, something designed to build them up, especially if you have traditionally considered them to be "beneath" you.

Consider your culture and the idea of superiority and inferiority? Were you raised to believe you were above someone or below anyone? Do you think it's time we moved on from this? Is this a conversation you would be willing to start with your family and friends?

We are *all* equal and valuable. The good thing is you can change your perspective if you wish.

BE A PERSON OF YOUR WORD

SELF-EMPOWERMENT

IF YOUR WORD IS NOT FIRM, then expect to feel the people around you reducing their circle of trust (**#Self-protection and the circle of trust**, *wisdom 68*), because why keep inviting someone who keeps breaking their word? Shrink the circle when that constantly happens.

We can resist giving into cynicism and deciding there's no point in honoring our word just because others don't. Hold to your word. Over a life span, you will find you attract the same quality of people as you into your world, and the added bonus is, they are people you can really trust.

REFLECTION INTO ACTION

When are you guilty of not keeping your word?

Pick one area in your life and decide to keep your word in that area. It may be social appointments, or it may be promises to call or to do something.

Focus on this area for a week.

Advanced: Pick another area. ☺

#74

SUPPORT THE YOUNG FIGHTERS

CLIMATE COURAGE

THESE KIDS CAN'T BE KIDS. They're scared for their very future, the future we adults are leaving them due to our apathy, unwillingness to see what is before our own eyes, and the greed and corruption that has seen endless growth without regard for its impact on the planet.

We are destroying the foundation of our ability to live, and they will experience the brunt of that. It's a miserable-looking future right now, if we don't change. As we've taken more and more of what we want, their future is offering them less and less.

IN SUPPORT

List 3–5 young folk you can support:

1.

2.

3.

4.

5.

MY COMMITMENT

What am I going to start doing to help in the fight for our collective children's future?

1.

2.

3.

4.

5.

DOMESTIC VIOLENCE AND FEAR

SELF-AWARENESS

THESE DAYS, WE KNOW that violence often comes from a place of fear. Though taking it out physically on a loved one is a line most of us won't cross, we all know feelings of anger and frustration. At a time when the fears that feed them are getting extra oxygen, a time when many of us are cooped up with those loved ones in a way we haven't been before, at a time while facing a very uncertain future. There's a lot to be fearful of.

So, when you feel your anger flare up, take a time out to dig deep inside. Try to recognize and name what you are feeling for what it is. Find a safe place to discuss it and ensure you don't misdirect it towards someone you love. That's an action you can never take back, and from which a relationship may never recover. When we can identify the feelings underlying our thoughts and actions, we can address them, rather than staying trapped in them. Self-awareness is key to navigating this crisis.

REFLECTION

Step 1: How are your fear levels right now, on a scale of 1–10, where 1 is good and 10 is off the charts? How about those around you? Are they fearful?

Step 2: Reflect. Dig deep. What else are you feeling inside? List it all out and consider it!

Step 3: Identify what you can do about these feelings, like speak with your partner or a best friend. If you are really struggling, is it time to seek professional help? Let's face these fears, because when we do, we can overcome them.

A TIME FOR REFLECTION

CLIMATE COURAGE

QUESTIONS FOR REFLECTION

WITH WHATEVER TIME WE CAN set aside for it, let's ask ourselves some searching questions and find the answers, together.

1. Are you happy with your life—family, home, community, and sense of achievement, contribution, and meaning? Even if you are, is it time for new directions?

2. Are you questioning the frantic pace of life we left behind? Do we want it to be like that when it's all over?

3. Are you proud of the company you work for? Is it contributing positively towards all life on earth, or is shareholder value overriding these needs? If so, what can you do to change it?

4. Do you believe it is time we demand business to change dramatically, to take into consideration the earth's finite resources and take responsibility for the waste left behind? What businesses—including your own, but also including those you patronize—can you begin to hold accountable?

5. Are we individually ready to face up to our part in the devastation and suffering going on in so many places in the world?

6. Are you wasting less, buying less, saying no to single use plastics, consuming less meat, shopping locally, and making plans to reduce your emissions?

7. Is your country polluted and full of rubbish? Are you ready to demand action from the businesses that have profited from it for decades?

8. Is it time to close the wildlife markets, while creating new livelihoods for those reliant on them for income?

9. What about overfishing and destruction of the seas? What's the real impact? What's the risk to us?

10. Are you working to be part of the solution to end inequality, in all its forms?

11. What parts of life from before should we get rid of? I want the false, egocentric, hero-worshipping, sales-pushing nonsense gone. I want us to be real, to be meaningful. What about you?

12. And to the parents, are we acting and doing enough to ensure our children have a beautiful future?

We face big challenges.

Will you join me, so we can face them together? Will you raise your voice to demand change—on social media, in your communities, in your company, and on any platform or stage that you have access to? Will you join a rising chorus demanding better for all life on planet earth? Will we do the best we can to ensure our children do not face the worst possible outcome of the climate crisis?

#80

RECONSIDERING WORK

CAREER THOUGHTS

TECHNOLOGY PROMISED TO MAKE our lives easier, and it certainly has in many ways, but with 24/7 digital access and work from home becoming more and more common, sometimes it feels there is no escape from work. Not to mention the fact that cultural codes about disconnecting from work can be very different around the world.

There are so many aspects of work that can be challenging for all of us, so many qualities of being in an organization that we struggle with, so the question we need to ask ourselves is—are we happy with it?

Are you asking yourself how you want to work in the future? Do you feel empowered to follow different paths?

You don't have to make any changes right now, but a little daydreaming and planning can't hurt.

HOME-PLAY

Would you like to work differently?

What does that look like for you?

Where would you like to do it?

What would need to change for your family?

What are some of the steps you need to take to make this a reality?

1.

2.

3.

4.

5.

6.

7.

8.

9.

10.

#82

THE GIFT
OF ALL
EXPERIENCE

SELF-AWARENESS

THE EXPERIENCES WE COLLECT as we travel through life, whether we perceive them as good or bad at the time, are a gift given to us as well as an opportunity to learn and grow—*if we choose to see it that way.*

Psychiatrist and author Elisabeth Kübler-Ross puts it like this: "The most beautiful people we have known are those who have known defeat, known suffering, known struggle, known loss, and have found their way out of the depths. These persons have an appreciation, a sensitivity, and an understanding of life that fills them with compassion, gentleness, and a deep loving concern. Beautiful people do not just happen."

We can become the kind of beautiful she's talking about too, regardless of our start in life.

HOMEWORK

Who do you admire that has suffered something similar to your own hardship?

Have they written a book, are they on social media, or have they created information you can dig into and learn from?

If they are someone you know or are connected to, can you speak with them and ask them to help you see the gift?

And finally, would professional help be useful to you? Never be ashamed to take this path.

An important note. This is not a quick fix. It can take a long time to break negative mental habits, so take your time and rest when you need to. Just remember to always come back and keep digging within to help you become the shining light you were put on this earth to be.

#85

BEG YOUR PARDON, DOLLY PARTON

SELF-AWARENESS

EXAMINING MY FEELINGS about Dolly Parton taught me this. When I notice that I have strong feelings towards other people, I try to understand which part of those feelings is about me and has nothing to do with them.

Once you start looking at your own judgments from this angle, it's amazing what you uncover.

We are raised to pass judgment towards our fellow humans freely, but we are seldom encouraged to reflect on why we feel that way. Are our ideas the only right ones? Are our ways of living and being the only acceptable ones?

When you notice negative feelings towards someone, check in with yourself. If the real reason has something to do with you, then you can own that and stop deflecting it onto other people.

If we all took this approach to judgment, can you imagine what a difference it would make in the world?

REFLECTION

When you were growing up, what part of growing up, if any, made you really uncomfortable?

Who is someone that you do not know personally, but you may have judged?

Do you still think you are right and fair in that judgement, or does it require some deeper reflection?

OTHER PEOPLE'S BUSINESS

SELF-AWARENESS

LET'S MAKE A DISTINCTION between gossiping and bitching. If you wouldn't mind being overheard by the person you are talking about, chances are you're doing no harm, though you can never be sure. We don't all have equally thick skin.

Keep it simple. Don't join in when other people gossip, bitch, or tear down another person—just say no.

This wisdom, though, is about the destructive, ripping-another's-life-apart sort of gossip, which I'll call bitching. This form of gossip is often inaccurate and even when it might be factually true, it's the telling that is hurtful and mean.

When you break free of the "bitching circle" (as my husband likes to call it) you will definitely be happier and more whole.

JOIN THE NO BITCHING FOR A MONTH CHALLENGE

The rules of the No Bitching for a Month challenge are simple. Keep in mind that they apply to our social media presence and online communities, too.

1. You are not allowed to criticize anyone for anything, and if you feel inclined towards bitching, you have to replace it with something positive, like, "She is an awesome person, who loves…"

2. You can't share any news that is derogatory towards anyone else, no matter what (famous people included). If you notice you want to slip up, and feel you must share it, come up with a positive or compassionate angle.

3. If someone in your life does something horrible, stupid, or insulting, be the bigger person. Walk on and smile; it's their issue not yours. Send them a bolt of loving light if you feel like it, just don't let them fester inside you.

ACTION THOUGHTS

Step 1: List down the people you see as the ring leaders of your bitching circle, or the people who seem to be initiating or getting the biggest thrill out of doing it. Put yourself down if it's you.

1.

2.

3.

Step 2: Carefully watch your community and keep an eye out for those who seem reluctant to participate. Draw them out and tell them your concerns, asking for their advice on how to approach the problem. List reluctant gossipers:

1.

2.

3.

Recognize that approaching your friends could create division within your community, but if you can convince allies to join you, together you can start to build towards change, even if it means leaving the gossipers behind.

Step 3: If it's possible, speak to the whole group. Tell them you don't want to be part of those types of conversations anymore, because they make you feel horrible inside. Embellish on the reasons that make sense to you and the people you spend time with.

PS: None of us are perfect, but a commitment to not speak badly of others lifts us all.

TAKE ON THE CHALLENGE!

I completed a month of no bitching. ☐

The challenge I overcame in achieving it:

The difference I've seen in myself:

A REMINDER OF THE RULES

1. You are not allowed to criticize anyone for anything, and if you feel inclined towards bitching, you have to replace it with something positive, like, "She is an awesome person, who loves . . ."

2. You can't share any news that is derogatory towards anyone else, no matter what (famous people included). If you notice you want to slip up and you feel you must share it, you have to come up with a positive or compassionate angle.

3. If a stranger is being stupid or insulting around you, walk on and smile, send them a bolt of loving light. Don't let bad feeling fester inside you.

4. For the advanced players, this includes your thoughts. You're not allowed to have negative ones. If one crops up, shake it loose. Monitoring negative thoughts is really a superb habit when you get into it. (**#Do you have voices in your head?**, wisdom 4)

STAND UP FOR YOURSELF

CAREER THOUGHTS

WHEN SOMEONE SPEAKS TO YOU DISRESPECTFULLY, *don't stand for it,* no matter who it is, what title they hold, or what their status level is relative to yours, in work or in life.

Whether it's a bully in the family, at school, or in the workplace, do not let anyone speak to you disrespectfully. Stand up for yourself.

While they may be shocked when you do, they'll respect you more. And demanding respect gains you something ultimately even more important: self-respect.

I promise you one thing: if you stand up to them, bullies will always back down. Most people bully from a place of fear or pain. Standing up to them helps them reposition, which is good for them, too.

REFLECTIONS

When has someone spoken to me rudely and I did not stand up to myself?

How did I feel when it happened?

What were the feelings coursing through my body?

The next time someone speaks to me, or someone I care about, disrespectfully, what am I going to do?

#92

NO REGRETS

SELF-EMPOWERMENT

IF YOU HAVE REGRETS, shake them off or just do that thing, but don't let them live within you, festering away into un-lived resentment.

Please if you're ready to make a change, remember, if it's not making you happy, it's time to reflect and think anew. It's a great moment to reconsider all aspects of life. It's a great time for change. It's a great time to remember that life truly can be beautiful.

TWO QUESTIONS TO ANSWER

What have you always wanted to do that you have yet to do?

When are you going to do it?

185

#94

LET'S ADDRESS SHALLOWNESS

SELF-AWARENESS

WHEN WE WANT TO JUSTIFY indulging in something shallow, we call it "brain candy." Ask yourself, if you ate as much candy as you spend time consuming fluff on social media, what kind of shape would your body be in?

This junk food for the mind is leaving us spiritually malnourished and creating pain.

Prioritize the information you take on board. If it makes you feel negative emotions towards yourself or others, it's not good for you and it's definitely not feeding your soul.

HOME-PLAY

Do a simple check-in today with these two questions:

1. How much of your time is spent on shallow content?

2. Did you do anything today that's driven by FOMO rather than by things that matter deeply to you?

Moving forward, keep an eye out for these two things . . . and gently, kindly reduce the time and energy you put into *splashing around in the shallow end of the pool.* Check in with what you value deeply (**#Integrity and values,** wisdom 8) and put more time and energy there instead. Feed your soul with beauty and inspiration. Feed it with service and giving. You will be thankful you did. Your life will be more rewarding too.

#95

DEATH REFLECTION

SELF-EMPOWERMENT

WHEN IT COMES TO REFLECTING ON DEATH, I want to encourage you to not be scared of it and think about how you'll feel when that time comes. Because who knows when it will come?

I've included a reflection process here to fuel your life *now*.

Use it to help you focus on living your very best life and to become the very best version of yourself. This should always be our goal. Shake off anyone or anything that won't let you live the life you want.

Do it from an intention of love, not fear. Accepting that we will all die is an important part of the cycle of life, but the goal here is to make sure we *live* in the first place.

REFLECTION PRACTICE

Step 1: Close your eyes and spread loving energy around and within you. Smile if you can. Relax. Then visualize your funeral—with you in a casket (open or closed), urn, or whatever else is culturally appropriate and aligned with your wishes—and ponder these questions:

1. Have I lived the life I wanted to live? Did I do it? Did I do it all?

2. Look at the people attending your funeral, are they the people you wished to see there? Who is a gift in your life? Who isn't?

3. How do people think of you at this moment? Have you left a powerful legacy where you touched people's hearts? Or are people ambivalent towards your contribution?

Step 2: Write down what comes up.

Step 3: Pause and reflect. Step back from what you've written.

Step 4: Decide the past does not define you.

Step 5: Set some goals for the path ahead.

Bonus Step: Let go of the people you saw who are not a gift in your life, even family members. Be brutal. Be courageous. It's your life, and you only have one. Give it your all and leave the world a better place than how you found it. That's a gift each of us can leave for future generations.

The best legacy is to have given it our very best shot while we're alive and healthy.

Practice note: Recognize the thoughts that have held you back from overcoming your goals. Break free of them. If you need to, hire a coach or a mentor to help you break free.

Whatever you do, listen to the insights that come through and then act on them!

#96

THE RIPPLE EFFECT

SOCIAL LEADERSHIP

TIMES ARE TOUGH. Challenges are everywhere. We need to see the challenges, create impact, and find solutions. Then we need to implement them so that things really change.

It's time to acknowledge that those who raise awareness are as important a part of the equation as the people who are coming up with solutions and strategies for change.

The role of influencers is to prepare the ground for solutions. Influencers capable of communicating clearly are capable of changing people's minds, their hearts, and can create momentum for investment in solving the crisis.

You and I have the ability to create positive ripples of change within the communities where we have influence, like a stone tossed into a pond. The more of us who take part and create ripples, the more people we reach.

The ripple effect is incredibly powerful, and it is critical for driving the awareness which creates change.

If you want to create ripples of change, how do you do it?

Step 1: You step into your voice and start sharing relevant and powerful information. You help raise awareness and speak out in your community—to people who love you, trust you, and believe in you.

Step 2: Keep doing this. If you can influence a few people in your community and they start doing the same in their communities, it's exponential—and that's powerful. The ripples of impact can only multiply!

HOME-PLAY

What topic do I want to speak out on?

How can I participate in a meaningful way?

Where can I participate to get my message heard—social media, speaking, within my company, or beyond?

What trusted information sources do I need to start following?

How often will I commit to sharing information with my community?

IN GOOD TIMES AND BAD, LOOK TO SERVE

CAREER THOUGHTS

WHY SERVE? Whenever I've engaged in service, I've received far more than I've ever given.

Many of us have been taught that life is about looking out for yourself—that a *me-first* attitude is the road to success. Some people are self-centered out of self-defense. Other people think that service is a distraction that will derail personal ambitions

They're missing the fact that relationships are the key to all success.

Whether you're an individual or a corporation, a mindset of serving your community matters and helps when times are good, and when times are bad.

When times are tough, serve. Serve your community in whatever way makes sense to you. There will be great riches for you, in the form of mutual support.

WHAT'S NEXT?

Step 1: Identify where you can be of service. In your community? In your bigger world?

Step 2: Reach out and serve. Join a committee, volunteer your time, set up video meetings with communities you can help. Look around and work out where you can serve. Make a note of what you're going to do next.

#99

SPEND TIME ALONE, IN SILENCE

SELF-EMPOWERMENT

SILENCE CREATES SPACE TO investigate our thoughts and beliefs. This is powerful practice toward self-awareness, and it helps with so many of these other wisdoms.

It is only in silence that we can define and clarify our personal values and to really get to know ourselves, without external input.

Dig deep into the silence of you. Don't be scared of it. There is so much wisdom there. So much opportunity for personal transformation. (**#Have you met your soul yet?**, *wisdom 37*)

MY COMMITMENT

I will dedicate .... every day to silence OR I will take time out of my life in silence, alone.

My silent place will be ....

My silent practice will include:

1.

2.

3.

I hope to achieve:

1.

2.

3.

REMEMBER
TO SEEK AWE

SELF-EMPOWERMENT

STUDIES SHOW THAT IF YOU take the time to be awed by the world we live in, you can be a happier person.[3] Awe or a sense of wonder makes you kinder and more loving, and your social behavior is elevated because awe helps you appreciate things greater than yourself.

3   https://www.apa.org/pubs/journals/releases/psp-pspi0000018.pdf

AWE INSPIRING

List as many awe-inspiring places or moments as you can remember—try and list 20 to start with, across all aspects of your life.

What can you experience where you are? Awesome moments are more than just travel!

Now list your top 10 bucket-list experiences to seek when the situation allows you to do so safely.

CAREER THOUGHTS

ARE YOU AWARE WHEN fear is driving you to say NO? What's it doing to your dreams and yearnings (**#Unleash the yearners**, *wisdom 65*)? Have an *aha* moment when you work out what that fear is, recognize it's playing with you, and decided to say yes anyway.

Yes to courage.

Courage is about making brave decisions, and sometimes saying yes is the hardest of them all.

I want you to ask yourself—what can you say yes to? What makes you squirm, but if you said yes, everything could change?

Side note: please, make sure you're able to say no when it's necessary, too!

HOME-PLAY

When I say no, what am I reacting to?

What could I say yes to (even if I am squirming inside)?

What's the dream that I would get one step closer to if I started to say yes?

ABOUT
ANDREA T EDWARDS

ANDREA T EDWARDS, The Digital Conversationalist, is a Certified Speaking Professional (CSP), and a globally award-winning B2B communications professional. She works with the world's largest companies on the transformation needed within to maximize business growth in our digital future. She is a change agent, provocateur, author, passionate communicator, and social leader. Andrea's book *18 Steps to an All-Star LinkedIn Profile* was added to two Book Authority's listings as the "100 Best LinkedIn Books of All Time" and "22 Best New LinkedIn eBooks To Read In 2021."

With *Uncommon Courage*, Andrea hopes to inspire conversations that change the direction of how we live.

You can join her for more insights with special guests on the podcast/LiveStream *Uncommon Courage* and at her Websites **www.andreatedwards.com** or dig into the section **www.Uncommon-Courage.com**